VOICES FOR VOCATIONAL ACCOMPANIMENT

Leading, Mentoring, and Learning from the Next Generation

Forum *for* Theological Exploration

ISBN 978-1-09839-503-2

*For all the mentors who walk with
the next generation of Christian leaders.*

Staff Contributors

Darlene M. Hutto

Reverend Darlene M. Hutto is an ordained itinerant elder in the African Methodist Episcopal Church. She is the director of experience design at FTE, where she has served since 2007. Reverend Hutto received a bachelor's degree in philosophy and religion from Wilberforce University. She has her Master of Divinity degree and is currently a Doctor of Ministry candidate at Emory University's Candler School of Theology.

Heather B.P. Wallace

Heather B.P. Wallace is a learning design manager at FTE. Since 2014 her work has focused on convening discerning young adults, granting support to organizations accompanying young adults, and reporting on FTE's learning from partners in ministry. She has a master's degree in social justice and community development from Loyola University of Chicago's Institute of Pastoral Studies. She is passionate about storytelling, which stems from growing up in East Tennessee.

Diva Morgan Hicks

Originally from Dublin, GA, Diva Morgan Hicks now lives in Peachtree Corners with her husband and two beautiful children. She manages social media and online communications efforts for FTE. After graduating with her bachelor's degree, she began working in the non-profit sector as a communications professional. She says, "This role at FTE gives me the opportunity to change the world by helping those who God has called to be servants, teachers, and leaders in the church."

Contributors in Order of Appearance

Kristen Snow

Kristen Snow is a faith leader, activist, and artist rooted in Philadelphia, PA. She has spent several years exploring theological formation everywhere except in seminary. You'll often find her learning about the Delaware River Watershed, metalworking with her partner's furniture business, or singing songs.

Claire Hitchins

Claire Hitchins is a white anti-racist dissenting-Catholic southerner called to tend sacred spaces where connection, healing, imagination, and justice-making become possible. She is blessed to design and direct Re/Generation, a mentoring and leadership program connecting young Catholic change-makers with each other and with elders to support them in their transformational work. Claire has a bachelor's degree in religious studies from the University of Virginia and is delighted to join the Master of Divinity class of 2023 at Vanderbilt Divinity School.

Glafira Lopez

Glafira Lopez grew up in South Whittier, CA and has a Catholic background. She attended the University of California, Los Angeles and graduated with a bachelor's degree in Chicana/o studies and a minor in labor and workplace studies. She is passionate about the work that empowers asylum seekers, immigrants, and young BIPOC to flourish spiritually and socially, and to deconstruct oppressive systems.

Natasha Patterson

Natasha L. Patterson is a Compassion-Centered Spiritual Health Chaplain Fellow with Emory University Hospital and a doctoral student at the Interdenominational Theological Center. Her current research examines speech and rhetoric as sources of spiritual and religious trauma.

Thiên Ân (Mary) Duong

Thiên Ân (Mary) Duong is an associate pastor of Maywood Church and a faith-rooted organizer. Born and raised in Sài Gòn, Viet Nam, she has long witnessed the power of faith communities in resisting oppressive systems, fighting for liberation, and embodying hope in society. Her undergraduate degree is in intercultural studies and business administration. She completed her Master of Divinity degree to learn spiritual tools and traditions to help sustain and empower communities for transformation in the face of violence and injustice.

Josh Lopez-Reyes

Josh Lopez-Reyes (he/him) is a son to Rocio and Manuel, brother to Abraham and husband to Grecia. He is a Californiano with family roots in the lands today known as México and the southwest of the United States. Josh currently serves as the director of the Echo Park Refugee Welcome Center (EPRWC). The EPRWC is a faith community for spiritual refugees and a resource center for political refugees.

Grecia Lopez-Reyes

Grecia Lopez-Reyes is senior community organizer with Los Angeles Alliance for a New Economy. Before this she served as a faith-rooted organizer for Clergy and Laity United for Economic Justice, focusing on labor and immigration work. She has a bachelor's degree in global studies, and a master's degree in transformational urban leadership from Azusa Pacific University. Grecia is also in the process of pursuing ordained ministry in the United Methodist Church.

Mark Mares

Mark Mares serves as the minister of youth and families at First Presbyterian Church in Ann Arbor, MI. Previously he served as a fellow for the Albany Synod Fellowship program in Upstate New York. Mark grew up in Holland, MI attending a small, Spanish-speaking Pentecostal church his grandpa planted in the 1970s, and is grateful for the role that small church played in his formation. He is a graduate of Hope College and Western Theological Seminary.

Chelsi Glascoe

Chelsi Glascoe is a multifaceted powerhouse from Silver Spring, MD. She has a bachelor's degree in sociology from Clark Atlanta University and her Master of Divinity degree from Mercer University. Chelsi serves as a collegiate chaplain in the Atlanta University Center, empowering young adults with truth and transparency. She is also the founder and chief operating officer of Social Shifter, a digital media marketing agency that caters to nonprofits and churches.

Jen Bailey

Jen Bailey is an ordained minister, public theologian, and national leader in the multifaith movement for justice. She is the founder and executive director of the Faith Matters Network, a womanist-led organization equipping community organizers, faith leaders, and activists with resources for connection, spiritual sustainability, and accompaniment.

Robert Chao Romero

Robert Chao Romero is a professor of Chicana/o studies and Asian American studies at the University of California, Los Angeles (UCLA). He received his PhD from UCLA in Latin American history and his Juris Doctor from the University of California, Berkeley. Romero is the author of the recently released book, Brown Church: Five Centuries of Latina/o Social Justice, Theology, and Identity. He is an ordained pastor. Romero and his wife Erica co-founded Jesus 4 Revolutionaries, a ministry to activists.

Tuhina Verma Rasche

Tuhina Verma Rasche lives a hyphenated life as a second-generation Indian-American raised in a devout Hindu household and is a follower of Jesus. She is an ordained minister of Word and Sacrament in the Evangelical Lutheran Church in America (ELCA) and is called to work for the representation of God's full diversity in the church.

Kelly Chatman

Kelly Chatman is advisor to the bishop of the Minneapolis Area Synod of the Evangelical Lutheran Church in America. He retired from pastoral ministry in 2020 after serving many years as pastor at Evangelical Lutheran Church of the Redeemer in North Minneapolis, and as director of the Redeemer Center for Life. He started the Center for Leadership and Neighborhood Engagement, a training institute to support congregations aiming to deepen their connections to the neighborhoods in which they reside.

Edited by Dr. Patrick B. Reyes, senior director of learning design at the Forum for Theological Exploration.

Special thanks to Kerry Traubert and Rev. Dr. Dori Baker for copy editing and the exploration of themes. Thank you to Angela Giles, communication manager for managing the design process, and gratitude for Beaver Design Group on the design of this piece.

Table of Contents

A Word on Mentoring
by Rev. Darlene M. Hutto

Then I heard the voice of the Lord saying,
"Whom shall I send,
and who will go for us?"
And I said, "Here am I; send me!"

— Isaiah 6:8 NRSV

You reached out...
In moments when we didn't always recognize
the struggle that called us together.
It was as if we knew that the mirrors of our
greatness would reveal the unknown.
Our connection was the key that unlocked
the door to our self-discoveries.

We began...
with an invitation by way of inquiry.
Whether by phone or perhaps in passing
we connected not as friends but rather
companions on a path toward excavation.

We interacted...
in the sharing of our experiences.
This invitation allowed us to take a look within
reflecting on what we could only hope to have
seen before.

We discerned...
asking that which was unknown in me to
merely become known in you.
The path of exploring together didn't require
us to become replicas of the other
but rather sojourners on a path engaging the
Genuine in ourselves.

We awakened...
into a place of recovery.
Now we are both seen.
Our invitation was always to see that which
you couldn't see, as you also see me.

You arrived...
both you and I, charting a pathway unknown
into new possibilities!

For now, we see in a mirror, dimly,
but now face to face.
Now I know only in part;
then I will know fully,
even as I have been fully known.

— 1 Corinthians 13:12 NRSV

This poetic reflection is a mirroring of the mentoring I've engaged in with young adults, FTE's grantees, and broader partners in the church and the academy. The mentor invites the mentee to see with new eyes and to reclaim their narrative as they discern that which they are called to explore. Mentoring is an engaged and a reciprocal discovery. It reveals that which is already present and at work in the other. We are better when we discern together!

Introduction

The Forum for Theological Exploration (FTE) has since 1954 supported young adults discerning a call to ministry. Through grants, fellowships, and gatherings connecting mentors and mentees, FTE has helped future generations of pastoral leaders find their vocations. *Voices for Vocational Accompaniment* is another tool to help support those who accompany discerning young adults.

This resource is presented in two main parts. The first section, "Young Adult Reflections on Vocational Accompaniment," lifts up the voices of young adults in FTE's network. Here they reflect on their experiences of being mentored and accompanied on their vocational discernment journey. Their contributions come in many forms, including essays, letters to their mentors, and poems. You will find that the diversity of formats matches the diversity of individuals and their experiences.

The second section, "Accompanying Change," features mentors and practitioners from FTE's network of faith-based institutions and congregations. They share their reflections on perfected methodologies and proven practices in their accompaniment and mentoring ministries. Themes around storytelling, community, and identity rise up again and again.

Woven between each of these sections and concluding the resource are interviews from scholars, pastors, and sages. In 2017, FTE's digital storyteller, Diva Morgan Hicks, sat down with Rev. Alisha Gordon, Dr. Gregory Ellison II, and Dr. Luther Smith to discuss mentoring. In addition to reading interview highlights here, you can watch videos of these interviews on our website (www.fteleaders.org) and on our Vimeo account: fteleaders.org/stories/lead-generational-change-for-good. Each interview is a gift wrapped up in a quilt of experiences and stories; they are treasures for anyone who opens these pages and receives them.

The resource is primarily designed as a guide for mentors in identifying key aspects of vocational accompaniment. However, any young adult in discernment who picks up these materials can easily glean a list of mentoring traits and qualities that they can use to identify a mentor—and to negotiate a meaningful relationship to accompany them on their vocational discernment journey.

In a report and reflection by Kiersti Phenow, a young adult who experienced an FTE Ministry Exploration and Mentoring project, she tells the story of how meaningful exploration of vocation can be when you are mentored, and when space is held throughout the process. While connecting with faith communities who use community gardening as a form of ministry and healing, she said, "I think that this experience has reminded me that church can and should be a place for transparency, a place that honors this most natural cycle of life, both human and natural creation, and our duty to be compassionate and curious towards both .... I would love to imagine ways that we can organically sit in our dirt, our compost, and know that it is all right to be there and it is sometimes the most beautiful and necessary process of rebirth." Phenow ultimately decided to enroll at Wake Forest's School of Divinity to continue her explorations and preparations for this ministry.

> "I think that this experience has reminded me that church can and should be a place for transparency."

FTE uses the word "accompaniment" as a way of naming the empowering and dynamic process that results and pours forth from those who journey alongside young adults. While throughout this work the term mentoring is used, accompaniment can mean so much more than mentoring. Vocational accompaniment is not a linear process or simply a relationship between a mentor and a mentee. It is what Phenow describes as sitting in the dirt, composting, and witnessing a rebirth. It is true cultivation of discernment, gifts, and calling.

For almost seven decades, FTE has journeyed with diverse young adults who are pursuing ministry. Our hope is that by lifting up the stories of this group of mentees and mentors, future generations will be inspired to pursue their calls—knowing that these sacred relationships, and the fruits of true accompaniment, will be with them every step of the way.

> Our hope is that by lifting up the stories of this group of mentees and mentors, future generations will be inspired to pursue their calls.

Mentoring the FTE Way
by Heather B.P. Wallace

At FTE we work with congregations, denominations, faith-based organizations, and communities to support and accompany young adults in their vocational discernment toward ministry. Several common themes about best practices come up in what we hear in reports and conversations. These have emerged out of years of trial and error, followed often by trial and success on the part of our network. The themes include Context, Holding Space, Practices, and Inquiring/Inspiring Questions.

Context is Key

Context is everything. Vocational accompaniment and mentoring are not a one-size-fits-all process. Discernment practices that work in one context or community may not be effective in another, and yet, having *the right mentor* in a *specific context* can make a significant difference in the results of a young adult's discernment process. A mentor needs to be open, affirming, and aware of the contexts of both the mentor and the mentee. This is especially important for mentoring marginalized young adults who are pursuing calls to ministry. We might think that it is common sense, but time and again mentors offer advice, programs, or support that is designed with someone else in mind. Finding the practices and people that are contextually appropriate for life-affirming discernment is the aim of good mentorship.

> Finding the practices and people that are contextually appropriate for life-affirming discernment is the aim of good mentorship.

Holding Space Requires Slowing Down

The young adults FTE encounters are busy studying, working, caring for loved ones, and serving their congregations and communities. The opportunity to hold space for them at discernment retreats—and connecting them with the right mentors who have time to create space for them—are both keys to their vocational discernment. The act of slowing down, reflecting, and being available to listen to the Holy within opens their hearts and minds to hear and see where they may be called. It is not about FTE or the mentors having all the answers. It is about giving young adults the space to search and find their calling within themselves and within their communities. Without that space and time for discernment amid the busyness of life, young adults might not have or take the time to clearly reflect on their gifts, and on where they might be feeling the tug of God's call in their lives.

Practices Build Reflexes

Vocational discernment is not a journey with an endpoint. It continues throughout life for young adults and mentors alike. Finding a set of practices that works for discernment can be like a toolbox that you go back to again and again, picking up the right practice for the right moment. Whether that is a Clearness Committee, an Assets Discovery Survey, a Beloved Communities Map, Spiritual Direction, or the CARE Practices, young adults have access to a variety of practices that they can either revisit or try. FTE curates resources and practices to help young adults and mentors alike. These practices and resources can help build the reflexes to discern together. Some are simple, like setting an intention for the day or pausing and reflecting on their gifts. Other practices take more time, like ancestral healing

> Vocational discernment is not a journey with an endpoint.

and learning practices from our traditions. What matters is creating access to a range of practices.

Inspiring Questions Prompt Next Most Faithful Step

When we accompany young adults at FTE discernment retreats and other events, we develop reflection questions that inspire them to think about their next most faithful step. Often the daunting part of vocational discernment is how big the idea of vocation can seem and how far into the future it might appear to be. Young adults often feel concerned that they have to have all things figured out all at once—when they really just need to have a first direction and identify their next most faithful step.

> Often the daunting part of vocational discernment is how big the idea of vocation can seem.

At one of our gatherings, two FTE Fellows sat down to reflect on their vocational journeys and where their next most faithful steps might be. Listen to Rev. Tyler Sit and Rev. Jennifer Bailey at fteleaders.org/stories. Five years later, Revs. Sit and Bailey are still serving their communities in new and transformative ways.

FTE offers this gift, a resource for vocational accompaniment. We hope it will serve both the young adults and the mentors and practitioners who walk alongside them on this journey to discover the next most faithful step toward God's calling in their lives.

Authentic Identity and Authentic Accompaniment
Interview with Rev. Alisha Gordon

The Rev. Alisha L. Gordon is a faith leader, preacher, and educator whose work intersects faith, culture, and politics. A native of Decatur, GA, Rev. Gordon earned her Master of Divinity degree from the Candler School of Theology at Emory University. She currently serves as a faith-based advisor for E Pluribus Unum Fund and is the founder of The Current Project, an advocacy nonprofit for single mothers in East Harlem, where she lives with her teenage daughter. She is the former executive minister of programs at the historic Riverside Church in New York City and served as the national director of faith-based outreach for the 2020 Bloomberg presidential campaign. Her commitment to the church is formed and informed by her practical approach to Scripture and social justice.

Note: The full interview has been edited for length and content.

DIVA MORGAN HICKS: How do you think the relationship with your mentor, Rev. Dr. Greg Ellison, has inspired you to lead differently, be innovative, or think outside the box?

REV. ALISHA GORDON: Greg Ellison is the consummate storyteller. He is always his most authentic self everywhere he is. He's always wearing his bow tie and his sneakers and his baseball cap because that is just who he is and he's that way in every space—whether it's here at Emory University or in someone's church or over in the hood in the West End of Atlanta. So my relationship with him has always taught me and liberated me to remain true to who I am; even in accepting the call to ministry to say, "Okay, well I'm going to preach

> ## "Lord, if I'm going to do this I need to be able to just be myself."

and I'm going to teach."

It was something that I didn't want to do because it came with so many expectations, often unrealistic expectations of me and what it meant to be a preacher and a teacher. My trade-off with Jesus was, "Lord, if I'm going to do this I need to be able to just be myself." I'm from Decatur. I grew up in a working-class family. I like to wear Chuck Taylors when I preach. I listen to trap music. All these things make me who I am. My relationship with Greg has always affirmed that it was okay to be me, whether it was here in an academic space or at church. Being able to model that, and the ways in which he creates space for other people—those are things that I've learned and taken on as a part of who I am. I know it's a direct result of my relationship with Rev. Dr. Gregory Ellison.

DIVA: How do you think the relationship that you and Rev. Dr. Ellison have has impacted you as you create relationships with potential rising scholars?

ALISHA: One of the things that you learn spending time with Greg is how to create space. That's what Fearless Dialogues is about. That is how he lives his life. He's always creating space for people to sit down and talk and he's a good listener. So when I'm engaging with students from the Youth Theological Initiative or different programs, I am always cognizant of the ways in which I'm listening for people's stories. I'm trying to hear what it is that they are trying to say. We're talking about seeing people differently, hearing their stories to create opportunities for change.

How do you create space for people, so that you can see them, fully see them, see them for who they are, see them for what it is that they bring to the table and hear what it is that they have to say? There are so many people that we come across that we are just in passing, ships in the night, and we don't take time to sit still and create space for people to talk and to share what it is that's going on in their life. Those are things that you pick up after working with Greg for three or four years; it becomes a part of who you are.

Especially working with young people whose voices are often unheard because they're young and people feel like they're inexperienced, you take that, and you model it. You put it into practice, and you see how it works for you in different circles. The ways in which you learn to navigate the world is a practical thing that you can take from space to space to space that works, because people are always looking for an opportunity to be heard.

DIVA: Can you tell me more about the opportunity for change that you hope for with your work or in your own personal journey?

ALISHA: Yeah. Sometimes, there's this adage that asks the question, "How do you eat an elephant?" The answer is, "One bite at a time." If you want to tackle the biggest of big problems, whether it is a social justice issue, an issue of ecology or terrorism or inequality in the church, inequality for women, inequalities for differently abled people, sometimes those issues seem so big and they are hard to bring down to a sizable way to manage. But I think what we have learned in our work together is that it really is about this notion of the "three-feet challenge."

Greg tells this story about how he was this precarious little boy who asked his auntie how he could change the world. His aunt said, "Well you can only change the three feet around you," which is probably about arm's length. That means one person at a time. It's hard to think about the very institutional ways that we need to change our world, but it's much easier, and easier to digest, if you think about it just one person at a time. How can I put myself in a position to use whatever privileges I've had to create space for you to feel empowered and to have a sense of agency to change the world around you? Just one person at a time.

DIVA: Why is mentoring so important to those in ministry and theological education?

ALISHA: Mentoring is important because it helps you navigate common issues and common pitfalls of ministry. There's so much wisdom in following the footsteps of someone who's already done it. It reminds me of the old Bugs Bunny cartoons where he's trying to navigate not stepping on the little landmines. It's easier for him to do that when he's following the steps of the person in front of him. Mentoring I think is even biblical. You think about Abraham, you think about Joshua, and you think about Elijah, and all these people had mentors in their lives that guided them in these really important and meaningful ways.

> Mentoring is important because it helps you navigate common issues and common pitfalls of ministry.

These were people who had already had these experiences, they were often people who had already had many failures in their lives. How do we cling on and create a mutual relationship with people who are older or wiser or more experienced with us and not only to just glean from them, but also to offer up something to their experiences as well?

It reminds me of the story of Elijah and Elisha. There was this reciprocity in their relationship—between mentor and mentee—that even though Elijah was older and much wiser, he showed Elisha something new about God and about their experiences together. Mentorship I think is as old as time; it's just the ways in which we begin to learn to navigate the world alongside somebody. I think even with my relationship with Greg, there's such a mutuality in the growth and the sharing that is really helpful and reciprocal on both ends. Greg's mentorship really shaped my life in this new way that hadn't happened before when I didn't have mentors—when I was just out here winging it and flying by the seat of my pants.

DIVA: Do you think these relationships help you create
opportunity for change or make a bigger impact for good
because more people are working together?

ALISHA: When you have a group of people who are mentors, that
means you have a shared interest; there's a shared common goal. Just
think about five mentor/mentee relationships with a set of influence
in a particular area, in a different area in a different part of the
world, a different geographical area, a different level of interest,
a different space of influence, and different socio-economic and
intellectual spaces.

Think about the ways in which that not only expands the ways we
create change, but how it really becomes exponential. Change can
really be explosive where you have a core number of people who
think alike and who have the same goal for change. It really can do
much more than one person can do alone.

DIVA: Do you think sometimes people don't even realize that
they're involved in mentor/mentee relationships?

ALISHA: Yeah, I do. I think about the first time I called Greg my
mentor. I hadn't thought about it that way because in a lot of ways,
outside of the classroom, we're peers because we work together
on these particular projects. For all intents and purposes, he is
my mentor because he's navigated the world in ways that not only
offer levels of wisdom, they are very parallel to the ways in which I
navigate the world.

The language of "mentor/mentee" does feel very formal and I think
it brings on a level of hierarchy sometimes, but I do think that people
are involved in those types of relationships who have absolutely no
idea that that's what it is. Maybe that's good. I've seen Greg in that
light in my life for a couple years before I actually even used the
language.

DIVA: Why do you think it's important to pay it forward as a mentor, to create relationships with rising young Christian leaders?

ALISHA: I think about all the wisdom and all the ways I've been exposed to great opportunities because of my relationship with my mentors. It would be absolutely selfish to not create that same space for other people. I think that is the way that we continue to have exponential levels of change. I can't say that enough. To just give back to another young Christian leader in the same ways that were given to me is the way in which we continue this snowball effect of enacting change in different areas of the world.

> To just give back to another young Christian leader in the same ways that were given to me is the way in which we continue this snowball effect of enacting change.

It may just be giving people access to your resources or inviting someone along to a particular event that they typically wouldn't have access to, but I think we all have an obligation to do that as Christian leaders, as members of community, because we're not an island unto ourselves. No one can say that any level of success is the result of their own work. It is always the result of not only God, but also people who have walked alongside us during this process.

DIVA: Do you think that could help influence or change the way that people, especially young adults, see the church as a place where they can see hope and make a change in the world?

ALISHA: There's all this conversation about how young Christian leaders are leaving the church, but I think oftentimes we navigate Christian life as individuals. That's important, but when we shift to think about change and hope for change and relationships in a reciprocal way, that perpetuates this communal sense of living life out together. The church can be a place where young Christian leaders can come and network and develop relationships with people who are wiser and older, or even their peers who may be the same age, but are a little further along the path than they are.

There also has to be an understanding from mentors that they have to be willing and ready to engage young Christian leaders in ways that are meaningful to them and create space for them and not put them off over in the Sunday school room or in the church basement. Creating space for them to be their most authentic selves and to know that what they have to bring to the table is valuable. Everyone can benefit from building themselves up as Christian leaders, as lay leaders, as community activists. How can you bring to the table what it is that you have to offer, and also create space for other people who are willing and ready to learn?

Living and leading change for good to me means to use your platform, whatever that may be, your level of influence, your sphere of influence, to push people to do and be better. Whatever that looks like.

> How can you bring to the table what it is that you have to offer, and also create space for other people who are willing and ready to learn? Living and leading change for good to me means to use your platform, whatever that may be.

I'm a teacher and I'm a preacher and I lead worship. I'm always opening my mouth to do these things. I think about the thousands of people that I have spoken in front of, or sang in front of, that had my heart been different I could have promoted evil, and I could have promoted bad ways of thinking about church and about God.

I recognize the power and the agency that I have to really shift the way people not only think about themselves but think about people around them. We have the power to promote that and to use our platforms for good.

DIVA: Dr. Luther Smith is one of Rev. Dr. Ellison's mentors. He mentioned your name to me as one of his students. That connection was really interesting to me.

ALISHA: Dr. Smith was my professor before Greg was; he was probably one of the first people here who affirmed my call to ministry. I'm just so grateful for him and grateful for his knowledge and wisdom. I was a fellow for a program here and he took five or six of us under his wings and always created space for us to talk about the ways in which ministry was calling us. I always felt like I had this really unorthodox ministry model to write and teach and travel that didn't look very institutionalized—it didn't seem like it happened just in the academy, or just in church. It was this hybrid of the two. Dr. Smith was one of the first people to really affirm that was possible.

For the full video, visit fteleaders.org/stories/lead-generational-change-for-good.

Young Adult Reflections on Vocational Accompaniment

These reflections from young adults look into vocational accompaniment and mentoring in two formats. One focuses on being mentored with a group of peers; the other reflects on one-on-one mentorship. FTE hears time and again how important it is to have mentorship in the discernment process, and how it can come in different forms with different benefits from each.

We Are the Ritual
by Kristen Snow

I n 2019 I embarked with a group of friends on an ambitious project to create a self-guided theological education cohort for nine months.

The learning journey was grounded in a ritual class guided by Rev. Rhetta Morgan. We met with Rhetta for the first time in July over video chat to assess if we'd be a good fit. I was immediately struck by her power and presence. She asked us discerning questions about our experience with ritual and faith, listening and responding as we each shared, crowded around one laptop. I felt a strong sense that we were about to begin a powerful spiritual journey, and honestly felt some fear and trepidation about the depths to which we would go.

> I felt a strong sense that we were about to begin a powerful spiritual journey.

From September to April we met once a month for a four-hour ritual session. Rhetta welcomed us into her small, beautiful home that shares land with a Quaker meeting house, a field, a cemetery, and a great oak tree. She called the class, "Ritual for Change Makers." She seriously committed to be our ritual guide for our time together. At each gathering, we set an intention for our time together, then moved into ritual-building. We started by grounding on the land we were on; sometimes we would pair up and lead each other, other times we would walk alone around the grounds, circling up and creating spontaneous rituals as a way to wake up our muscles and our minds. We would then move into a time of checking in. The check-ins became an important moment for Rhetta to get to know each of us individually and for us to bring whatever burdens we were carrying to the group. She would listen and encourage, telling us in times of disappointment, pain, or disillusionment that we are the ritual—that we can respond and grow from wherever we are.

After our check-ins, Rhetta would often move into a time of teaching, sharing from her deep wealth of knowledge as a spiritual leader. She taught us how to perceive the world as a ritual platform. She gave us diagrams and graphics outlining what tools we needed to develop to lead more fully in our communities. She gave us homework for the next month. During the second half of our class time, we presented or shared. We wrote songs, we wrote and practiced rituals together, we looked into our ancestral roots for grounding in ritual practice, we built altars and, most importantly, we practiced the art of spontaneous ritual, pulling from inspiration within to lead the group.

Rhetta taught us how to move a crowd in times of agitation, how to capture a moment of grief and to hold it, how to use our own instincts and awareness to tap into a deeper sense of connectedness with God and with each other. We were able to apply these skills directly to the COVID-19 pandemic. Working together as a group of newly trained "ritual for change-making leaders," we created a grief ritual to help guide people to process and engage the grief that has come up during the loss and fear of the pandemic.

As a mentor, Rhetta is nurturing, insightful, and generous. She offers her wealth of gifts openly, asking in exchange that we take ourselves and the work of ritual building seriously. She would often tell us that "we are the ritual," which we all found to be extremely uplifting, especially from a teacher who is so experienced and wise. Rhetta is vulnerable in her teaching. She would weave stories of her own life and experience into the teaching, sharing struggles as well as triumphs in her own journey of life and ritual practice.

We came out of the experience with many tools, including a ritual notebook we each created, with many songs and many prayers. We came out more connected to God, to each other, and to the earth.

Embodying the Priesthood
by Claire Hitchins

As part of a learning journey to explore my call, I traveled periodically to visit with other Catholic women called to priesthood.

Between these stops on my pilgrimage, my mentor Anne and I would meet up for half-day retreats to pray and reflect on my experiences. At the time, I saw my travel plans as central to my discernment; the mentoring was a welcome but somewhat peripheral addition. Four years later, I cannot remember many details of my travels without looking back at my journals—but the memories of Anne's mentorship have shaped the way I live my vocation each day since then.

I remember one of our early retreats. I showed up expecting to report back on the conference I had attended and instead found myself telling my whole life story. The candle we lit burned down as my call narrative tumbled out, awkward but eager to be spoken at last.

I remember the time I challenged Anne on what I perceived to be her submission to the oppressive authority of the Roman Catholic Church. In response, she challenged me to open my mind and heart yet wider. My lofty ideals and theories got brought down to earth that day, planted into the ground of human experiences, relationships, and transformations in all their nuance and complexity.

> She challenged me to open my mind and heart yet wider.

I remember the time we met up on a Sunday. Anne brought a seedy multigrain loaf of bread and a small jar of wine and asked me if I wanted to consecrate the Eucharist. I breathed deeply and felt a warm breeze on my face as I told the story by heart and lifted my hands over the elements in celebration and blessing.

While my travels that year certainly expanded the horizons of my vocational imagination, Anne's mentorship offered the sacred space for me to weave those experiences back into my own story. They brought the learning home. She gave me the rare gift of mutual mentorship in intergenerational friendship. We learned from each other and with each other, each honoring the unique wisdom and perspective of the other.

> My call isn't somewhere out there waiting to be discovered, but resides right here in my own being, ready to be lived more fully.

Perhaps most significantly, Anne affirmed the ways I was already embodying the priesthood I sought, reminding me that my call isn't somewhere out there waiting to be discovered, but resides right here in my own being, ready to be lived more fully.

Honoring the Gift of Accompaniment

These reflections honor the gifts that mentors bring to their relationships. In particular, they lift up the trailblazing of women of color in ministry, whether in the formal pulpit or in the home and community.

An Ode to the Women Carrying the Good News
by Glafira Lopez

My thoughts, my yearnings, and my convictions are all a mixture of the people who have impacted me.

The saying holds true: It takes a village to raise a child, especially a child in faith. If we are to be like children, it will take a village to help us get there. In this walk with God, I thank the women of faith in my life, mostly women of color, who have shown me how to love justly, and who have called out the works of God in my life.

To the women who raised me and gave me life: You showed me what it was like to depend on God. You covered me in your prayers so that I would be safe, provided for, and well. You had faith that a roof would be over my head and that food would be in my belly. I saw your prayers answered by God, and I learned to pray to him for provision like you did. To you, I owe my confidence that God is the father who cares for me more than the birds in the air and sees me with greater value than those.

> In this walk with God, I thank the women of faith in my life, mostly women of color.

To those who showed me how to love like God: I remember entering college not knowing real friendship, and not knowing what it was like to be loved intentionally. I missed my family back at home, but you took me into your family as if I were special. You reached out to me as if I were worth pursuing. Ultimately, you showed me what it was like to live life with the purpose of following God by loving his children. At the same time, although this was your ministry, you showed me that the goal to love people like God was not disconnected from the friendship that we formed. To you I owe the transformation of my understanding of what it is to pursue people with love, and to be pursued by God.

To those who showed me to love myself like God loves me: You were in my life during a crucial season. I was in a pit with so many painful things going on at home. I was extending love left and right, but you reminded me how deeply and passionately God loved me, how deeply he wanted me to be loved, and how deeply he wanted me to love myself. To you I owe my understanding of how God doesn't just want us as his workers extending love, but how he wants us to be loved abundantly. From you I learned that God does not neglect the part where he says love the Lord your God and your neighbor as yourself.

> You exemplified what it was like to commit all your acts and your future to the Lord.

To those who showed me how to dedicate my life to God: You exemplified what it was like to commit all your acts and your future to the Lord. To you I owe my understanding of what it means to follow God and know that he has a purpose for our lives that is much larger than what we could ever imagine. Your lives have taught me that he is a God that thinks beyond generations and has a purpose for us all.

To those who called me in when I needed to be called out: I grew up thinking that being called out meant a criticism on my character, but you showed me that it was an invitation to do better and to be better. In the moment it stung, but in the long run it helped me be a better person. You showed me that God, in his graciousness, calls us out and back in when we are in sin.

I thank those who showed me that to love God is to live justly, walk humbly, and speak up for people who are marginalized. Thank you for giving me the guidance in understanding that God is a God of justice, that he sees me and my story, and that he cares deeply for people who are marginalized. Your testimony of God's empowerment in your life and your deep faith in him despite your margins have shown me the goodness of God. This created in me a desire to love and trust God despite my circumstances. Thank you for showing me what it is like to walk with God in bringing about justice. Because of your modeling of this, I have been able to experience God in such a profound way and understand new depths of his love.

> Thank you for showing me what it is like to walk with God.

I have been blessed to be mentored and discipled by women who understood the love of God and shared it widely. You have shown me what it is like to be a woman from the margins, transformed by God, and bravely carrying the good news of a resurrected God to a hurting world.

There are No Shortcuts
by Natasha Patterson

"I light my candle from their torches."

- Robert Burton, *The Anatomy of Melancholy*

This is one of my all-time favorite quotes. I've always associated it with the idea of mentorship.

Mentors hold an invaluable resource that can illuminate the trajectory of one's path. As I glean from their wisdom and experience, I will develop a light of my own that will carry me through life's journey.

As a Black woman in ministry, there are no shortcuts. There is no secret formula for bypassing the hurdles and resistance encountered because of ethnicity, gender, or systemic understanding of what it means to be a preacher or pastor. However, there are loosely constructed maps from the recollections of those who embarked on the voyage before me.

For this reason, I have had professors, chaplain educators, and pastors who have graciously agreed to mentor me and to share with me the intimate narratives of their successes and their failures. My pastor is the epitome of a great mentor, a confidante, and a friend. Our relationship was not merely one in which she told of the grandeur of her success as a professor, pastor, academic administrator, and elder in her community. Rather, she conveyed the honest truths of her lived experiences, the struggles that she endured, and the hardships she overcame to be the person she became. One of the many things that I respect most about her mentorship is that she never assumed to know what it was that I needed.

One afternoon we met for lunch, and she simply asked, "What is it that you need from me?" Out of all the mentors that I've had over the years, no one had ever asked. I think there is some subconscious assumption that if one is "further along," whatever they offer is what you need. But by her posing the question, we were able to clarify what my expectations and needs were in that season of my life. As it became clear that the seasons of my life had changed, she would ask that question again. I didn't always have an answer readily available, but it encouraged me to begin reevaluating what I needed.

I have been blessed over the years to have had numerous mentors who have both poured into me and have challenged me to become my best self. In high school, I was encouraged to find the person doing what I wanted to do and to learn from them. That's exactly what I did. I have been forever changed by their guidance, knowledge, and expertise. For that I am grateful. And as the flame on my candle grows bigger, it is my duty to help light the candles of others.

> We were able to clarify what my expectations and needs were in that season of my life.

Mutual Mentoring: Mentoring Across Difference

This reflection is from the perspective of mentoring across difference. It reveals how mentoring relationships are not one-way streets but can be mutual. Young adults who find those deep relationships can acknowledge the gifts of their mentors, elders, and peers, but are often comfortable enough to reach back and lead their mentors into unexpected conversations and learning.

A Sincere Letter to a Mentor
by Thiên Ân (Mary) Duong

Dear G.,

You are one of a few mentors with whom I feel safe to share many parts of my story because you have vulnerably shared your story with me.

Our relationship started with you being my educator for my first unit of Clinical Pastoral Education (CPE[1]). I knew you were a gifted educator, and I had the privilege of being under your mentorship for two consecutive CPE units. However, I did not fully realize the subtle and thoughtful ways you had shaped me until I had other educators on my CPE journey. One of the greatest gifts you shared with me was your vulnerable leadership. You welcomed my peers and me into your home, shared your story with us, both the joys and heartaches, and created such a hospitable space for us to share our stories with one another. You taught me by example to lead with an open and tender heart. I brought up to you many questions related to my experience as a Christian Asian woman about the imbalanced power dynamics allocating to race, gender, class, age, and religion in the U.S. society that permeates in our medical setting. You were the only one among all my CPE educators (who also happened to be white) who chose to lean in to discomfort, asked

> I don't remember a time when you were defensive or dismissive of my questions or experiences.

[1] Clinical Pastoral Education is interfaith professional education for ministry. It brings theological students and ministers of all faiths (pastors, priests, rabbis, imams and others) into supervised encounters with persons in crisis. Out of an intense involvement with persons in need, and the feedback from peers and teachers, students develop new awareness of themselves as persons and of the needs of those to whom they minister. From theological reflection on specific human situations, they gain a new understanding of ministry. Within the interdisciplinary team process of helping persons, they develop skills in interpersonal and interprofessional relationships. *(As defined by ACPE.edu)*

questions, and sought understanding. You told me later, after my units with you ended, that you never had a student who challenged your leadership so much. However, I don't remember a time when you were defensive or dismissive of my questions or experiences. Instead, you were humble to acknowledge what you did not know, and to apologize when you realized that you made assumptions. You modeled for me a different kind of leadership and a different way of being in the world: openness and vulnerability. As a person who grew up in a culture of performance and perfectionism, I learned from you that it was okay to fail, and that my vulnerability could be a gift to others instead of a liability.

> I learned from you that it was okay to fail, and that my vulnerability could be a gift to others.

With a nurturing spirit, you brought out the best in me and called me to my potential. Though you had never heard me preach before, you gave me the opportunity to share a Christmas homily at our hospital in my first CPE unit. I was amazed at how much you took risks with me. You encouraged me to discover the gift of who I am by giving me freedom and opportunities to share myself. You advocated for me to have scholarships to join in the CPE programs when you knew I needed them. You introduced me to every opportunity you saw that might be beneficial to my personal and professional development. Every time I was in your presence, you made me feel as if I had everything I needed to do anything to which I was called. You saw the light in me and made space for me to shine. G., thank you for seeing me and for continuing to invest in me even when I am no longer your CPE student.

I know that you desire a flat leadership structure and try to create it with your vulnerable, approachable leadership. However, in the hierarchal CPE program and medical setting, you cannot dismiss that you hold a positional power that has significant influence on your students. When you deny your authority over your students, it blinds you from seeing the full impact of your actions on those under your leadership, especially with people of color who often defer to those in authority. I noticed that your love for equal power sometimes hindered you from seeing the current reality of power hierarchy. It limited you from embracing your power to hone it for the good of others, as you would like.

As you educated yourself about race and white privilege, I observed that you started "racesplaining" to my peers and me, many of whom were students of color. This might not have been your intention, but to me it came across as condescending. I have learned that without locating oneself properly in the race conversation, especially for white people in authority, one could unintentionally set themselves up as a white savior.

A white savior is one who sees people of color as victims of oppression and feels the need to "save" them—instead of dignifying people of color by amplifying their voices as those with agency to speak and to lead our community toward positive changes. I know it is your dream to contribute to the liberation of our world. That is why I hope you will have opportunities to receive mentorship from people of color as you continue to grow in your leadership in our changing world.

I look forward to seeing you again in person soon.

With gratitude,
Your Mentee

Mentoring through Identity

Mentoring for vocation can come from both traditional and nontraditional places. Though many people look to the church or to education institutions, our mentors also come in the form of our families, communities, and those who help us discover and embed our authentic identities into our authentic callings.

To My Mentors
by Josh Lopez-Reyes

To My Mentors
Young and old
In a world that is about individualism
You taught me to be myself, to love myself
To value familia[2]

Not just the familia that I was born into
You taught me what to do and what not to do
Who to be and who not to be
To be a puente[3]

Jamie, you taught me that even if you are oppressed
The goal in life is not to achieve the sueño americano[4]
This only further contributes to the oppression of others
And there is no correlation between the Gospel and prosperity

Ulisses, you taught me the true definition of being an entrepreneur
It is about paving a way, otherwise the change that we need to see
will never be
You showed me how colonization can affect our theology
And that is often necessary to decolonize our minds

Robert, you have introduced me to the myriad of beautiful Brown
prophets
This great cloud of witnesses, ¡¡Presente!![5], has prepared the way
Resisting slavery, machismo[6] and other xenophobic demons
In order to affirm the beloved worth of all creation

---

[2] Family

[3] A Bridge Builder

[4] The American Dream

[5] Invoking the presence and spirit of the name/s called.

[6] Patriarchy

Alexia, you showed me how to take our theology to the streets
To be a moral and prophetic witness
And that by ourselves we can only do so much
Because, el pueblo unido jamás será vencido[7]

Lydia, you paved the way for movement chaplaincy
Your organizing work turned an important page in our raza[8] history books
Although the work of dismantling white supremacy is beyond our lifetimes
You taught me that it has to start with our own

Rocio, you birthed me into being
I am who I am because of your abundant love
Above all, you taught me to love others

And that I can only love others in the bridge building, divine dance

Ched and Elaine, you have taught Grecia and me how to partner in the struggle
To have the imagination to think and work at the intersections
That we can't do it all, but that we all have to do
What we can, when we can, because, ¡Sí se puede![9]

---

[7] The people united, will never be divided.

[8] Latinx People

[9] Yes, we can!

Mentors in My Vocational Journey
by Grecia Lopez-Reyes

I n life we come across mentors, or spiritual guides: people who teach us important values that shape our understanding of life.

As a child who grew up in Guatemala, I see that my grandmother planted the roots of my vocation through her life of simplicity, compassion, and service to others. Her compassionate and fierce character instilled in me the importance of always standing alongside the community and fighting for change. I left Guatemala in 1996, but decided to return as a student in 2010. The people who I came across during this journey inspired my vocational commitment to social justice and human rights work.

When I first began to explore my vocation, I went back to Guatemala to connect with my roots and to explore my identity as a Guatemalan-American. I began to work with Trama Textiles, an association of 400 Mayan indigenous women that started in 1988 because of the Guatemalan Civil War and genocide against Mayan communities. This civil war lasted for 36 years, from 1960 to 1996; the period from 1978-1985 became known as la violencia (the violence). The U.S.-backed military regime under the leadership of General Rios Montt launched a counterinsurgency campaign against the guerrilla forces, claiming actions of anti-communism. This marked a period of tremendous state violence against potential subversives or communists, specifically targeting Mayan indigenous communities.

This war killed and "disappeared" mostly men, leaving countless women and children deserted, displaced, and alone. Trama Textiles was created by the many women who had to become the sole providers of their households. These women formed this association using an ancient Mayan tradition—backstrap weaving—to find ways to sustain their families and communities. Oralia Chopen and Amparo de León are two of the incredible women who led this association and mentored me through their leadership and stories.

While in Guatemala, I thought I would find mentorship in a professor or church leader who would share an abundance of political and social knowledge about the country. But I developed a deeper connection to these grassroots indigenous leaders. They invited me to their homes and communities, sharing their wisdom through their stories and experiences. Today in Guatemala it is said that those killed during the war were buried with their eyes open and survivors were forced to bury their memories with the dead. Despite the pain and trauma encountered, communities and leaders took collective action to resist this violence and systemic oppression. Oralia and Amparo taught me about the emotional, economic, and physical effects of the massacres and the disappearances that impacted their communities. They were left with trauma, pain, terror, and chronic poverty.

> Through their stories I was able to apply their wisdom into my life.

Amparo opened up to me about the challenges she has faced as a grassroots leader. She experienced threats against her life, beatings, and financial and physical exhaustion. Despite such challenges she would always say, "nunca pare de luchar" (I never stop fighting), for the love she felt for the women in her community. My desire to know them on a deeper level allowed me to open up my heart as a listener. Through their stories I was able to apply their wisdom into my life. They revealed to me the meaning of luchar (to fight or to struggle). Luchar is a simple word that I had heard all my life, but its meaning to me became more evident and transparent. Henry Nouwen writes that, "…a word can heal pains, bind wounds, and often give new life."

I realize that my mentors' acts of resistance and resilience came from that connection between suffering and a yearning for justice. Their stories and life experiences reminded me of my grandmother's example of determination, courage, and resilience. They also confirmed my vocational commitment to fight against the powers that be. Their stories awakened my heart and soul.

Their stories awakened my heart and soul.

Returning to Guatemala also allowed me to discover my family's own story. Prior to this journey, my parents never spoke about the internal conflict that happened in Guatemala. Silence is a tactic that has been used to control and suppress communities. I now learned that my mother had taken part in the student uprising during the internal conflict. She worked as a subversive, involved in organizing students for demonstrations to inform the public of the government's assassinations of local activists and indigenous communities.

This was an awakening for me and it revealed my own identity as a *Guatemalteca* (Guatemalan woman). I am thankful for the incredible women from Guatemala who have inspired, mentored, and encouraged me to embody resistance, faith, and resilience.

Letters of Gratitude From Those Who Have Stepped into Ministry

Each of these reflections is filled with the gratitude and thanksgivings of a mentored young adult who has now stepped into their calling. While sharing in these moments of gratitude, listen for the aspects of mentoring that you want to receive or want to provide.

A Letter from a Grateful Minister on the Vocational Journey

by Mark Mares

Dear Miriam,

"How are you?"

Every conversation we had would begin with this simple question. As I imagined in my rural context what a Ministry Exploration and Mentoring Project would look like, I knew I would need someone who understood what I experienced. You not only modeled for me the vocational ministry of a pastor, you invited me to embrace that calling as well. Our conversations were so valuable to me as you walked alongside me, and as we talked about both the joys and the sorrows of pastoral ministry.

Your questions always came at the right moment. They spoke to something deeper within. Sometimes they were piercing, but always in a way that invited deeper reflection and space for curiosity. In our conversations, it always felt like you created space for me to sit with those questions. I remember one time being struck by a question and we sat in silence. I remember your words clearly, "Silence is okay. We don't have to be anxious about the silence. Let's sit in it for a bit." This time and space opened me up to a greater understanding of the pastoral vocation and the call to be a follower of Christ, to and with a particular people in a particular place.

> This time and space opened me up to a greater understanding of the pastoral vocation and the call to be a follower of Christ.

As much as I am grateful for our mentor-mentee relationship, I am just so grateful for you—and the friendship that was forged through our time together.

I am where I am, in part, because of the many conversations we've had, the time I spent with your family, the time I've spent with you dreaming, laughing, crying, and carrying on during the Ministry Exploration and Mentoring Project. You opened yourself and your family to me. You showed me the importance of loving people in all of life's circumstances, building relationships both in and outside of the church, the importance of faithfulness, and participating in Christ's work of reconciliation. More simply, in showing and inviting me into your life, I've seen the importance of living in community, sharing in the love of the Triune God, a love that is dynamic and self-giving.

> In showing and inviting me into your life, I've seen the importance of living in community.

Miriam, I am so grateful for who you are and for your willingness to engage in this process. I'm grateful for your questions. I'm grateful for your wisdom. I'm grateful for the generosity of your time. I hope this letter finds you well, and your ministry life-giving.

Grace y paz,
Mark

A Letter to A Life Changer
by Chelsi Glascoe

Dear Life Changer,

As I reflect on our time together during my Ministry Exploration and Mentoring Project, I wanted to take a moment to "give you your flowers" and honor you with my truth about your impact on my life.

I take it seriously when I consider trusting someone with my vulnerabilities and my time, ears, and heart. So, during my vocational exploration, it was very important to me to identify a mentor who I admired and respected, and that was you. I watched you for years as you embodied the wisdom of our ancestors, the wit of a fox, focus, professionalism, balance, and, most importantly, love of God. This inner glow transcended into your role as a non-profit leader and change agent in Black and Brown communities, and I aim to do the same. When you accepted my request for mentorship, I was thrilled, but it did not always remain so peachy.

During our one-on-one discussions, I appreciated that you were honest, raw, and relatable. I learned some uncomfortable things about myself that stretched me to do more work than I originally bargained for. As we dissected my experiences during the Samuel DeWitt Proctor Conference, you challenged me to speak up on topics that made me uncomfortable, even if the entire room disagreed. Not only that, you shared with me the unforgettable story about how you took an unpopular stance in your college years, and although it went unrewarded, you went on fulfilled. I will always remember that.

> I learned some uncomfortable things about myself that stretched me to do more work.

What's funny is, while shadowing you in meetings and having sessions where we chatted about current events, school, and other topics, there were many things that I disagreed with. Much of your theology and many of your political views are completely different than mine! But because you gave me the space to articulate myself, and to be bold in the face of someone I revere, I have found a renewed confidence to preach the word of Yahweh—instead of deferring to personalities. You have always respected me. You challenged me to study harder, think differently, and be open. Thank you for the push.

> You challenged me to study harder, think differently, and be open. Thank you for the push.

At the end of the Ministry Exploration and Mentoring Project, I realized that I've always known I wanted to serve millennials as a preacher. The new information I learned was that I lacked the boldness required for the job. I allowed my personal insecurities and fright of the world's opinions to silence me. Your radical honesty about your pitfalls and perseverance confirmed that God can use me, too.

This project was a success not because of the information and knowledge I gained, but because of the personal development and spiritual transformation I went through that you supported via text, phone, social media, email, and birdcall!

Thank you for candidly sharing with me and for showing me better than you can ever say. I appreciate your time, but most of all I honor you for your example. You have showed me how to stand up, to speak up, and when to sit down. I will go forth in power because of it. It is well.

Signed,
Grateful

Mentoring and Being Mentored

Interview Highlights
with Rev. Dr. Gregory Ellison II

The Rev. Dr. Gregory C. Ellison II joined the Candler School of Theology faculty at Emory University in 2009. His teaching draws primarily from his work with Fearless Dialogues, the nonprofit organization he founded. Fearless Dialogues creates unique spaces for unlikely partners to have hard, heartfelt conversations on taboo subjects like racism, classism, and community violence.

Ellison's research focuses on caring with marginalized populations, pastoral care as social activism, and 20th and 21st-century mysticism. He is the author of *Cut Dead But Still Alive: Caring for African American Young Men, Fearless Dialogues: A New Movement for Justice,* and *Anchored in the Current: The Eternal Wisdom of Howard Thurman in a Changing World* with Westminster John Knox Press.

Note: The full interview has been edited for length and content.

REV. DR. GREGORY ELLISON II: I was sitting in class one day. As I was talking it sounded to me as if the words coming out of my mouth were ancient. They were not of me. I regard myself as a mystic. It truthfully scared the living daylights out of me, because as I was talking I could feel the students around me healing in some ways. It was almost as if I had their hearts in my hand. It scared me so much that I stopped mid-sentence, said "Let's just take a break," and left the room. I recognized at that point that something was growing in me that I needed some guidance on. How do I live with this unique skill set that seeks to heal communities, and that makes people feel vulnerable and open around me?

What I started doing was praying for my Yodas. I'm a fan of the Star Wars series; I felt in some regards like Luke Skywalker, that I had this force, this gift that I did not know how to harness, and so I prayed for these mentors, these leaders, these Yodas that could help guide me. Over the course of about nine months, five Yodas showed up. These were best-selling authors. One is a 95-year-old poet. The other is my dear friend Luther Smith. The average age of these Yodas is mid-60s, early 70s. They say, "Greg, we're here to support you, but while you are younger than us in age, you experience some of the same struggles that we encounter, and so we view you as a peer." That was really striking to me considering that chronologically these folks had been around in this world much longer than I. One of them asked, "Greg, how old do you feel on the inside?" In that regard, they have viewed me in some ways as an apprentice, to prevent me from stepping in the potholes, but also as someone they can learn with and from. It creates more of a partnership than a traditional mentoring relationship.

When Luke Skywalker went to Yoda he had to go to a swamp. An unlikely place to learn from a wise sage. One of my mentors lives in Madison, Wisconsin. The other lives in the hills of north Georgia. These are older white folks. The third is a woman who lives in inner-city Indianapolis. In a very, very rough neighborhood. Gratefully one is very close, and that has really kind of helped to forge a more familial relationship. I actually take the journey at least once a year to those various swamps to sit with my Yodas, and to learn with them.

DIVA MORGAN HICKS: What do you say about the importance of having those relationships, especially in the context of theological scholarship?

GREG: I think the thing that's coming up now is the long-term impact. It awakens dormant hopes that one might not be cognizant of. They help to put a finger on issues of fear and self-doubt that may otherwise inhibit my impact during this lifetime. It's also very pertinent to think about the fact that I am a part of their legacy. I live by the philosophy that the work that we do today will affect my great-great-grandchildren who are not yet born. My grandfather would often say, "We sit under shade trees that we did not plant, and drink from wells that we did not dig." I recognize that I am the beneficiary of their sacrifices and the struggles. In the same regard I have a responsibility to do the same for future generations, just as I have conversations with my mentee, Alisha, about vocation, and discernment, and activism, and how to incorporate education into community engagement. The work that we do collectively will have a long-term impact that we cannot yet see.

> The work that we do collectively will have a long-term impact that we cannot yet see.

The work that I do with Fearless Dialogues is all based on generational change. It's grounded in the belief that relationships change generations. Of course, policies can affect people in a lifetime, but if I am in relationship with a drug dealer, and he and I have the opportunity to sit face-to-face and talk about his life decisions, and talk about my life's journey, or if I'm in conversation with a foundation owner who has a billion dollars in their account, and I talk to them about my story and they share their story, over time something small happens inside of them: A seed is planted.

It may not take root, but I am of the belief that I don't have to take full responsibility for the total change of an individual life. That's God's responsibility. I scatter the seeds. I break ground with my shovel.

I feel like I have been the beneficiary of wisdom imparted by folks. They planted seeds in me, and I carry around my Johnny Appleseed pack, and try scattering those seeds in other folks.

DIVA: If you think about your work with Fearless Dialogues, what do you want that impact to look like in someone's life years down the road? If you could design that, what is your hope?

GREG: I'm a storyteller. We were working with a corporate group, and there was an older white man in the room. We had about an hour with this group, and the gentleman just frowned. I mean literally just frowned, and Fearless Dialogues is really kind of evocative, and we create spaces for folks to engage in these hard questions. He just frowned at me the entire time, and then about 45 minutes into our hour session his brow kind of softened, and he said, "I want to say something." I welcomed him to share it with the group. He said, "You know, I'm in my mid-'70s now, and I'm a titan of my industry. When I say stuff, people move. They jump, but I'm recognizing as I get older people don't move as fast when I say something. They don't jump as high anymore. Maybe I'm becoming invisible. Greg, is this what those young Black men in Ferguson feel like?"

For this corporate executive, this titan of industry, who makes decisions that affect huge numbers of people, for him to have that question to scratch consciousness level heightens his awareness. I believe it will impact the decision-making in some small and significant way. The broader vision of Fearless Dialogues is to scratch the subconscious of leaders. We look at the word leaders very broadly. Leaders could be folks like this titan of industry, but they also could be the candy lady at the end of the block who makes sure all the kids get to school. It could be the secretary at an institution like this, who interacts with students so that they pay attention to the people who may be unacknowledged around them. As you shift how people view the world and view others around them, you begin to alter how a community sees itself and those around them. I think that's meaningful work. It's slow, but the tectonic plates are moving slowly beneath the ground, and creating change and shifts.

DIVA: Why has Dr. Luther Smith's mentoring to you—and your mentoring to Rev. Alisha Gordon—been so important to you

GREG: Mentoring is so important. The people who have taken me under their wing have said, "Greg, you're so different, and it's okay. You're different, and because you are different you can create a change. You're different, and I was, too." You don't get stronger lifting feathers. You have to be vigilant in embracing all of who you are, and incorporating that not only into your scholarship, not only into your service, but how you live and move in the world is much more of an example of what you teach than what you write.

A spiritual teacher of mine said to me last night, "Greg, your sole responsibility on this earth is to inhabit yourself." I said, "That seems very selfish to me. That is my sole responsibility?" She said, "Your sole responsibility on earth is to inhabit yourself." She said, "Greg, the oak tree must be the oak tree. The walnut tree must be the walnut tree. The sun must be the sun. Sun, please don't be the moon. Out of all of eternity, you are the only one who has been created with your unique skill set. Therefore, you must take residency within yourself, because if you do not inhabit yourself we miss everything that you could give. We miss it, and we need you."

Good mentoring challenges people to inhabit the fullness of themselves. Alisha's a great singer, but she's also a great writer, and a great mother. She's also a very outspoken activist, but I also know her as a quiet and compassionate soul. For me to peg Alisha as just a singer, and say,

> Good mentoring challenges people to inhabit the fullness of themselves.

"Follow that dream," and push her in that direction...or to say, "Oh, you're a good theologian," but to not draw upon her gifts as a poet, as a writer, in many ways that would be a detriment to her. And so following the lead of wise teachers who have encouraged me to inhabit myself, I seek to help other folks who are different to occupy the fullness of their gifts, and to take up residence in their uniquely God-given abilities.

I live by several mantras. One of them is, "the longest journey you take in life is the trip from your head to your heart." Leading and living for change is an internal journey that manifests itself externally in the world, but if you're not in fearless dialogue with yourself what you do will not have the kind of impact that it could if you really are in deep conversation with who you are as a person. I think that's what my mentor was talking about.

Luther kind of took an interest in me very early in my time here at Candler. We actually were roommates during a faculty retreat. We got to see another side of each other. It's different when you see your colleagues in their pajamas. One of the things that became clear to me, and was a clear identifier that I could trust this man, is that he shared with me not only his own anxieties and vulnerabilities, but from day one he would say, "Greg, we want you to be successful. Not successful here. We want you to *thrive*." And so when he and I talked, our conversations did not start with, "How are your classes going? How are students doing in your classes? How are you negotiating committee responsibilities?"

We got to that, but the first question he would ask is, "How's Antoinette? How are your kids? How's your relationship at home?" Then we would end up talking about our families, and he'd share about his family. Luther is Howard Thurman's protégé. He's one of Dr. Thurman's students. He embodies this groundedness and quietness in his spirit even when there's chaos around. He and I believe in the intentionality and vigilance it takes to live an undivided life. By focusing on what it means to be a whole person, not just a good teacher, he modeled what mentoring is and should be.

DIVA: What would the world be missing, what would you be missing, if those mentoring relationships did not exist?

GREG: Dr. Thurman says, "It is a strange freedom to be adrift in the world." He talks about the need for mooring—someone or something to tether your life to. The most dangerous people I met when I was working in the prison setting were people who feel as if they have no sense of accountability to anyone. For me, a life without mentoring is a life untethered. My mentors, they push me forward. They affirm me, but they also say, "You really need to check yourself, Greg. You really need to take a deep and probing look at why you're making those decisions. In your writing. In your teaching. In your life."

> A life without mentoring is a life untethered.

To live a life without that type of constructive criticism, affirmation, and love of people who have lived lives as different people their entire life brings up feelings of isolation and despair. Depression. Apathy. Loneliness. I can call these people, and the folks in my Jedi Council at any time of day, and they may be a little upset for the first few minutes that I woke them, but then they'll say, "It's okay, what's going on?" It matters to have someone say, "We've been through this. You're going to make it through," and to offer some strategic ideas on how to navigate the terrain. To have wise voices like Luther who have navigated institutions for 30 years-plus, you can't put a price tag on that.

DIVA: Do you think that these mentoring relationships lead to innovation and create change for good?

GREG: Well, I think one of the beauties about praying for these Yodas is around this question about innovation the people that I have taken solace in as mentors are multidimensional. Mari Evans in Indianapolis, she's a playwright, a poet, a musician. She's done television broadcasting. She's a mother. A grandmother. Creativity oozes from her being, but she doesn't fit neatly into a box. Luther helped to start the Interfaith Children's Movement here in Atlanta. He's worked with L'Arche. With folks with developmental disabilities internationally. With the Children's Defense Fund. All while teaching, and pastoring, in an unconventional sense.

Innovation is often fostered in communities of innovators. I know that if I have a bold idea I can share it with my mentors and peers. Folks that I'm in partnership with bring their own set of skills and resources and gifts that push my innovative envelope—and so we work together in that endeavor. Change for good is a lifelong journey.

For the full video, visit fteleaders.org/stories/lead-generational-change-for-good.

Accompanying Change: Mentoring and Holding the Space for Discernment

Those who accompany young adults on this journey of vocational discernment have a tough, but beautiful role. They are present and hold space and make practices for the explorations of God's call in young people's lives. In this section, four practitioners explore best practices for accompaniment from their contexts.

Practices
by Jen Bailey

For communities across the United States, 2020 was quite the year. The global COVID-19 pandemic raged. Racial justice uprisings called attention to police and state violence following the murder of George Floyd. Our political landscape became increasingly polarized and fraught. All this together leaves little doubt that history books will be processing for many years to come the experiences we are living through now.

> The hard work of this moment is to create space to become quiet enough to discern how God is uniquely calling you to respond.

Against the chaotic backdrop of a world made undone, we as Christians are called to be messengers of radical hope. Ours is a resurrection hope that can see possibility where others see insurmountable challenge, to see new life where others see death. I believe in my core that the Gospel invites us into a place of imagination as active participants in God's larger work of justice and reconciliation.

The hard work of this moment is to create space to become quiet enough to discern how God is uniquely calling you to respond in this season.

In 2015, my friend Nicholas Hayes and I created and piloted a resource dedicated to helping young people leverage their life story as a roadmap for vocational discernment. To us, vocation is not synonymous with a job or role. Vocation, in our understanding, is a matter of articulating your prophetic purpose in your own words.

In today's lingo, "prophecy" is often associated with predicting the future. But in the biblical tradition, a prophet is someone uniquely attuned to the present, one who reads the signs of the times. More specifically, the prophet gives voice to the tension between the world as it is now and the world as God dreams it to be. A prophet clearly sees and feels the brokenness—the injustice—of the world as it is. But a prophet also keeps faith in the potential for the world to be healed and transformed by the coming of God's justice. Anger and grief, on the one hand, and passionate hope, on the other, are the two sides of prophecy.

Each of us has a prophetic vocation. We are called collectively to live in spaces of grief and hope, so that we might become partners in God's work of justice and reconciliation. Yet each of us also has a unique role to play. To find it, we must read the signs of the times for ourselves and discern where the Spirit most moves each of us to act. What specific part of the world's brokenness most speaks to you? To your own passions, griefs, hopes? Where do you feel most called to do the work of justice?

A key insight we gleaned as we piloted this project with young adults is this: While one's job or role can change, their prophetic purpose often remains consistent over the course of a lifetime. Discovering our prophetic purpose anchors us in our ability to reflect and understand our own story and the stories of the people, places, and communities that have helped shape us along the way.

The Bible is full of famous prophetic call stories, from the uncertainty and reluctance of Jeremiah (Jeremiah 1:4-19) to the supernatural splendor of Isaiah (Isaiah 6:1-8). Most often these narratives involve the prophet

> Look at the ways God calls us in those moments of awakening and respond to that call through the choices we make.

hearing the audible voice of God and being directly commissioned into service. Sometimes our prophetic purpose is revealed through these obviously spiritual experiences, like those recounted by the biblical prophets. But more often, it comes from the powerful, everyday experiences that "wake us up" to the brokenness of the world. One way, then, to understand our prophetic purpose is to look at the ways God calls us in those moments of awakening and respond to that call through the choices we make.

As you begin to explore your prophetic purpose through the moments that shaped and still shape you, here are a few questions that might be helpful:

> 1. When was your first experience of injustice? How did the experience change your worldview?

> 2. Describe a moment, recent or long past, when you witnessed an act of injustice that broke your heart. How did you respond to your anger?

> 3. When was a time you believed you could make a difference on the issue that broke your heart? What actions did you take? How did you know God or others were with you?

When we take the time to examine these transformative moments of call and response that have inspired us, we see themes emerge. Perhaps you have always had a passion for caring for God's creation, or for offering radical hospitality to strangers. Maybe you have always had a tendency to speak up for those denied a voice in certain halls of power. Whatever it is, know that God is with you and will never leave or forsake you.

Finally, a word on roles. In my own ministerial journey, I find that making the distinction between prophetic purpose and role is incredibly important—even liberating. Societal norms tie our sense of call to the jobs we hold. As a result, we allow our self-worth to be wrapped up in our ability to be productive in these positions. Some of us will be blessed to have these two things—our job and our prophetic purpose—align for a season. But in my lived experience, there are few things that are as certain as change. As we progress through the life cycle, our responsibilities and those to whom we are accountable will necessarily transition. Parental figures age. Our health status changes. We may choose to partner, raise children, or not. These life cycle shifts do not mean we need to abandon our prophetic purpose, but rather assess and discern how our purpose might be called to manifest differently in each new season. You might be called to the front lines of protest now, and into more of a support role later in life. It's all okay.

One of the beautiful things about being a Christian is the constant reminder that it is not up to us alone to solve the great challenges of our time. Rather—as we seek our prophetic purpose amid the pandemics of virus, injustice, and political division—we might take solace in these words, often falsely attributed to the great freedom fighter Archbishop Oscar Romero:

> We cannot do everything, and there is a sense of liberation in realizing that.
>
> This enables us to do something, and to do it very well.
>
> It may be incomplete, but it is a beginning, a step along the way, an opportunity for the Lord's grace to enter and do the rest.
>
> We may never see the end results, but that is the difference between the master builder and the worker.
>
> We are workers, not master builders; ministers, not messiahs.
>
> We are prophets of a future not our own[10]

May it be so. Amen.

---

[10] First presented by Cardinal Dearden in 1979 and quoted by Pope Francis in 2015.

Practices
by Robert Chao Romero

"The proclamation of the Gospel (kerygma) and the demonstration of the Gospel that gives itself in service (diakonía) form an indissoluble (indisoluble) whole. One without the other is an incomplete, mutilated (mutilado) gospel... From this perspective, it is foolish to ask about the relative importance of evangelism and social responsibility. This would be equivalent to asking about the relative importance of the right wing and the left wing of a plane."

— C. René Padilla

During the 1960s and '70s, Latin American "evangélicos" went through a phase of spiritual deconstruction and reconstruction, much like what is occurring among many Christian young adults in the United States today. Though they ministered among Latin American university students, evangélicos like René Padilla and Samuel Escobar were originally trained in an individualistic American gospel. It emphasized personal forgiveness and heaven but possessed little spiritual imagination for social transformation. They brought back an individualistic American gospel to Latin America but were often met with blank stares. In the crucible of the revolutionary Latin America of the 1960s—where thousands were "disappeared," and hunger and poverty were the norm, university students replied, "Why is this good news to me and family? How does this gospel speak to the fact that my father was killed yesterday by the U.S.-backed dictatorship and my family has nothing to eat?"

This led Padilla, Escobar, and others on a path of theological and vocational exploration which culminated in the framework of "misión integral." According to Padilla, misión integral is "the mission of the whole church to the whole of humanity in all its forms, personal, communal, social, economic, ecological, and political." As with Latin America five decades ago, misión integral, or, holistic mission, offers an important model for our accompaniment and vocational discernment practices today.

Padilla's reference to "two wings" is the key. Our accompaniment and vocational discernment practices must be grounded in both wings of the Gospel airplane. Jesus wants to transform every aspect of our lives and the world. Nothing and no one is left out. In my experience, most Christian churches or organizations tend to emphasize one wing or the other. They emphasize either one's personal relationship with Jesus detached from the grave social ills of the day, or social justice without personal transformation in Christ. They focus either upon the verbal proclamation

> Our accompaniment and vocational discernment practices must be grounded in both wings of the Gospel airplane.

of the Gospel or the embodiment of Christian hope in acts of justice and compassion—but rarely both at the same time. And so, the plane of American Christianity is in a tailspin. And thousands are choosing to self-eject.

If biblical mission is indeed all encompassing, our accompaniment and vocational discernment practices must also be grounded in both wings in very practical ways.

Wing One: It may seem obvious, or simplistic, but Wing One (personal/vertical relationship with God) is built up through the cultivation of a life-giving and transformative relationship with Jesus—through Scriptural reflection, individual and corporate prayer, fasting, spiritual direction, service in the local church, pastoral counseling, and therapy. Because many of these important practices have been traditionally misrepresented and weaponized, they need to be reclaimed, reimagined, and reintegrated into the lives of those we accompany in creative and loving ways. If our personal character does not match our talk of social justice, the plane will crash, and we will bring lots of people down with us.

Wing Two: To develop a strong and healthy second wing, our mentees need to go beyond theory and social media activism and get dirt under their ministry fingernails. Most of the real work of social justice is neither glamorous nor glorious, and involves muscles of deep commitment, personal relationship, and discipline which many have never been challenged to develop. Faith and biblical truth are learned from our sisters and brothers of marginalized communities as we follow their lead in the hard work of ministry together over a sustained period of time. There is no substitute. Many people read books and tweet, but very few actually show up. Day. After day. After day. And, as we say in the Brown Church, the sheep get suspicious when the shepherd doesn't smell like sheep.

Practices
by Tuhina Verma Rasche

In my roles as a pastor, facilitator, and mentor, I often find myself returning to the first chapter of John's Gospel to reaffirm my Christian faith. Part of that reaffirmation is in the mystical opening verses of the Gospel, which read, "the Word was the beginning, with God, and was God." I also cling to my own adaptation of this verse:

And the Word became flesh and lived among us, and we have seen this glory, the glory as of a parent's only child, full of grace and truth.

If the Word took on flesh and bone and came to dwell among the entirety of God's created world in a tumultuous time—if God came to dwell with us in such a way—then I am led to believe again and again that the entirety of our being truly matters. The words that create our lived experiences, the words that form our personal stories, matter deeply to the Word. Yet as a pastor, facilitator, and mentor, I then wonder, how do we create meaning in these words? How do we embody the words that create our life stories and experiences? When we gather in communities, how then do we interpret and honor the words of these shared stories? How do we viscerally and incarnationally respond to our words and to the words of others?

> How do we embody the words that create our life stories and experiences?

God shows us that words have power in their meaning, with the Word taking on flesh in the person of Jesus of Nazareth. Our words continue to have power today, yet I feel there has been a sense of carelessness with deeply powerful and unsettling words. I attempt to work with communities to establish baselines in the hope that people do not talk *past one another*, but instead *to each other*. This is much of the work I do in the denomination into which I've been ordained, the Evangelical Lutheran Church in America. I speak to predominantly white groups about equity and community building (or lack thereof). I present words and phrases to the community, and as gathered as Christ's body, the Word made flesh, we attempt to find meanings that resonate within the body of the community. The words and phrases are deceptively simple; some members of the community scoff at the simplicity, but once conversation and wrestling with our words and meanings begin, what was once deceptively simple becomes a tangle of lived experiences, bringing with it different interpretations and embodied forms of meaning. Some of those deceptively simple words and phrases include power, racism, equity, justice, forgiveness, and reconciliation.

> Many people are often talking past one another or at one another, rather than one another.

In discussing these words, many people are often talking past one another or at one another, rather than to one another. This is holy wrestling, to move from the objectification of words to the embodied and lived experiences of the Word, which then bring a multitude of meanings. When trying to find a communal sense of meaning, many people have brought their lived experiences with these words. The lived experiences vastly differ with one another, bringing with them a cacophony of narratives in the struggle to find meaning.

When personal narratives are brought to the community of Christ, the meanings of these words oftentimes shift, change, and expand. Yet there is not one sole meaning. It would be unjust to force one sole definition for an entire community. To do such a thing would be an act of violence, to detract from not just a person's lived experience, but also their incarnational being. Many have had to contort and deform their lives to fit a colonial, dominant narrative.

That dominant narrative brings with it an either/or structure with no room for a spectrum, no room for a life to be lived in-between spaces. A dominant narrative tells us all sorts of awful things, that if you do not conform or buy into this dominant narrative, your words, which form your stories, your body, and your life do not matter.

As someone who loves how words are used—and as someone who believes that the Word made flesh came to dwell among us in the person of Christ—I also realize that there are consequences to the words we use (and those we do not use). I am also at fault for words used and words omitted; I continue to struggle and to learn and re-learn. I realize that words have power, and sometimes that power is oppressive and does not liberate. Words can give power to a segment of the population and victimize other parts of humanity, and there are times where we don't even realize how entrenched we are. This is an imperfect work for an imperfect time.

Even in the midst of imperfection, we continue to wrestle, stumble, and find ourselves in new places that cannot be confined and constrained to a single meaning. This is where the wideness and beauty of liminality reveals itself. In this cacophony of lived experiences, of bringing meaning to words that are so deceptively simple, we must find ways to be community together and to create communal meanings of how to be the entirety of Christ's body. Liminality also reveals that sometimes meanings are not etched in stone; the communal meanings of words can shift and change, becoming more expansive in its interpretation. When embracing liminality, an apocalypse can take place, a great unveiling into not just the wideness of God's grace and mercy, but also the wideness and meaning of the words we use with one another and the

> We must find ways to be community together and to create communal meanings of how to be the entirety of Christ's body.

experiences we share in story with one another. An opportunity is provided in this apocalypse to not just share stories with one another, but to weave together the words of those stories—to wrestle with the meanings of such words, and where those meanings converge and diverge in a tapestry of communal storytelling.

The words that create our narratives are a holy part of our incarnational being, just as the words of our siblings are holy. In facilitation and mentorship, this is the opportunity to be freed of the binds and constraints placed upon us by others. This is an opportunity to live with not just one meaning, but to struggle with and possibly embrace a diversity of meanings. What continues to give me courage—as a facilitator and mentor deeply rooted in the Living Word—is the variety of meanings and interpretations in which God reveals Godself to each of us, whether that be through the Holy Trinity or through knowing that our neighbor is created in the holy image(s) of God, and that we continue to be woven into the Word and the expansiveness of God's tapestries.

[1] *John 1:14, adapted from New Revised Standard Version.*

Practices
by Kelly Chatman

I grew up in a city where, as a youth, I attended a church within walking distance from our home. My summer routine included hours of play and activity with other boys in my neighborhood. If church was a regular part of the life of my friends, somehow that never came up as part of our conversations. What did come up was the full court gym at my church. My friends somehow knew that my church had a full court gym where we could be safe and play basketball. My friends and I loved to play basketball in my church gym. And I loved the fact that I had the power of connection to make this possible.

My pastor and his wife lived next door to the church. The process to access the church gym went like this: I would call my pastor and ask if we could come to the church to play basketball; my friends and I would then walk to the church, and my friends waited while I went next door to the pastor's house. I then rang the doorbell and waited for the pastor to come to the door. Each time, the pastor had me wait until he returned to give me the keys to the church. My pastor entrusted me with the keys to the church.

The practice of accompaniment and vocational discernment is the time-honored discipline of entrusting to young people the keys to the church. And I'm not referring to the church building. I'm talking about key practices that offer meaning, hope, and purpose to our youth. My pastor practiced accompaniment when he entrusted me with the keys to the church building, while letting

> The practice of accompaniment and vocational discernment is the time-honored discipline of entrusting to young people the keys to the church.

me know he was paying attention each time I asked for them. He walked with me on my journey to becoming an adult.

My own career working with young people started outside the walls of the church, when I was recruited to serve as an adult volunteer for the congregation's weekly neighborhood outreach. I had graduated from college and lived in pursuit of fame and fortune. With that in mind, I recall thinking to myself, "What am I doing volunteering my time with a bunch of young people?" But that didn't last long, because before I knew it, I was hooked by the work. I discovered a passion for working with young people that would lead to roles as youth director, coach, teacher, chaplain, pastor, and director for youth programs for an entire denomination.

Years earlier, that church recruiter had extended to me the opportunity that would open the door to understanding my passion for working with young people. In doing so, she supported my own vocational discernment process.

In my experience, best practices in accompaniment and vocational discernment begin with the realization that young people have amazing gifts to offer. Often those gifts are yet to be discovered. As adult advisors, we share the opportunity to accompany young people in their faith and vocation discovery. But practicing accompaniment and vocational discernment is more than understanding what it is and deciding to do it.

Here is my list of best practices:

Caring: I am not sure where I first heard the aphorism, "People don't care how much you know until they know how much you care." I believe that demonstrating caring to young people is a critical core value to the practice of accompaniment. We cannot fake caring.

Relationship: If there is a universal practice in the accompaniment of young people, it is the commitment to relationship. Because relationships are the epicenter of a young person's world, investing time and getting to know a youth or young adults—their hopes, dreams, aspirations and struggles—is the portal to meaningful relationships. It's important for adults to view the chance to accompany youth and young adults on their vocational journey as a unique and wonderful opportunity—not as a currency we can use to buy our way into trust. In many ways, relationship and accompaniment are the same. In the context of community and social settings, relationship is a primary way to understand our belief in God. How does my life consistently display a faith that shows up in how we treat others?

Trust: If relationship and authenticity are building blocks, then trust is like the mortar in the practice of accompanying young adults. The gateway to a relationship is trust accompanied with consistency. Consistency builds trust. Young Life Ministries has a time-honored saying, "You have to earn the right to be heard." As adults, do we do what we say we are going to do? Do we show up when we are needed and when it is inconvenient?

> Trust is like the mortar in the practice of accompanying young adults.

Intergenerational Welcome: Congregation is the most powerful institution in the world. At their best, congregations offer the practice of disrupting the isolation of young adults traveling as a "tribe apart" from other generations.

No other institution states that no matter who you are or where you come from, "You are welcome in this place." Still, churches are challenging and inefficient settings for the practice of accompaniment for young adults because, for them, there are many rules that limit access, power, and influence. At the same time, churches provide critical access to ritual, community, and retreat—all with the potential for intergenerational encounter.

Authenticity: Authenticity is a highly held value among young people, who watch and observe how and if we as adults communicate authenticity. And it's easy to confuse being authentic with being "cool." I think of authenticity as "keeping it real" and being willing to pay the price of being who we really are. Young people also pay attention to how well adults treat others, so we need to practice how we are equitable in our encounters with people, especially people being ignored or treated unfairly. In social contexts, the value of authenticity translates into the cost of discipleship, being willing to stand up for what we believe in.

Equity and Justice: Taking a stand for equity and fairness is important to young adults, particularly in relationship to race, gender and sexual preference, and identity, where people have experienced systematic injustice. Unfortunately, youth and young adults tend to exercise this practice in the streets more so than in churches where they must navigate the bureaucracy of rules, procedures, and unrecognized systems of white supremacy. Among the myriad of young people who marched in response to recent police violence and abuse are young people awakening to their vocations and hungering for accompaniment in discerning how to live them out.

> Among the myriad of young people who marched in response to recent police violence and abuse are young people awakening to their vocations.

Community Organization and Leadership Development: Investing and equipping young adults with leadership development opportunities is a nuanced focus for faith leaders. For previous generations, attention was given to functions within the church, such as leading worship and teaching Sunday school. Today, leadership extends into the neighborhoods. It includes enriching lives through non-profits, community organizing, social ventures, and use of social media. In Minneapolis, for example, a local congregation operates a retail bike and coffee shop managed by young adults. The mission of the bike and coffee shop is to train local youth to become bicycle mechanics. This practice combines accompaniment and vocational discernment with a positive impact on the community by employing young adults to train and equip local youth in their job readiness.

These are a just few among many best practices of accompaniment and vocational discernment for youth and young adults. I believe the heart of these practices is our willingness as adults to entrust young adults enough to "give them the keys" with the same confidence someone once invested in us.

> The heart of these practices is our willingness as adults to entrust young adults enough to "give them the keys".

Accompanying the Next Generation
Interview with Dr. Luther Smith

 **D**r. Luther E. Smith, Jr.'s current research focuses on the writings and correspondence of Howard Thurman, advocacy on behalf of children, and a spirituality of hope. Smith is an ordained elder in the Christian Methodist Episcopal Church.

In 2009, Smith received the Phillips School of Theology Bishops Thomas Hoyt and Paul Stewart Institutional Ministry Award for Outstanding Service to the Ministry of Academics. In 2010, he was the recipient of Emory University's Emory Williams Distinguished Teaching Award. It is given in recognition of the important role of classroom teaching in collegiate and graduate education.

Smith has his PhD, Saint Louis University, 1979; MDiv, Eden Theological Seminary, 1972; and BA, Washington University, 1969.

Note: The full interview has been edited for length and content.

DR. LUTHER SMITH: With the Civil Rights Movement, I became very aware of how transformation occurs for individuals beyond the signing of a bill or even beyond some kind of change in policy in a community because of protest. The very process of seeking change can be transformative, and hopefully celebrated by giving persons a sense of self in a way that perhaps they had not had before, a sense of who God is in the struggle, a sense of what makes us a people, a beloved community. That was very important to me.

More recently, I've been involved with the issues of children in poverty and children involved in the juvenile justice system and children who are sexually exploited. We were lobbying for a child-oriented bill down at the state capitol building. The woman next to me, after she was finished speaking to a legislator, turned to me and said, "I have never done this before. This feels good." As much as we were there to address the empowerment of children and their needs, that was an example of an individual who experienced something transformative in this process of seeking change that would benefit the larger community.

I think all of us are looking to navigate matters of vocation, job, and faith with others. There is something about pursuing these matters alone that leaves you isolated and questioning in ways that you know are not beneficial to you, and not beneficial to what you're trying to accomplish. I think mentoring has really enabled us to affirm the significance of relationships in all that we do. I think we were created by God for relationships and for relationships that nurture us, sustain us, enable us through conversation, to ask questions, to be guided in particular ways, to find our own voice. There's an empowerment that comes for individuals through being mentored. It is the sense of, "I have a companion on this journey."

> I think all of us are looking to navigate matters of vocation, job, and faith with others.

I think it's one of the gifts of some organizations that insist that you have an "accompanier" on your journey—someone with whom you can talk about your questions, such as what's going on in an organization, what's going on within you in terms of how you're functioning in a leadership role, or how you're functioning in a follower role. It's those aspects of having a mentor that can really give someone a sense of capacity. At times, I'm desperate for feedback. Mentoring allows that. Otherwise, I think it's very easy to experience the despair of aloneness. It's very easy to try to compensate for that despair of aloneness by asserting your authority, when perhaps you're actually questioning or wondering *about* your authority. I think there's some real fundamental gift that comes through mentoring that relates to the very character of the human spirit.

DIVA MORGAN HICKS: Can you tell me about someone you considered to be your mentor, who helped guide you along in your vocational journey?

LUTHER: There are many people. I continue to hear their voices—not because we had a formal mentoring relationship, but because there would be occasions when I would be in conversation with them about something that was important to me. They would say something that I suspect, for them, was not even considered a major offering. It was probably a side thought for them, but it struck me as something that I would remember for the rest of my life. It made a difference as to how I looked at things.

I think that can be a gift of mentoring: not that you have someone who's coming with all of the answers and all of the experience, but someone who can just engage you in conversation. That's part of the miracle of relationship and of presence. It works in formal mentoring relationships, but for me, it has especially worked in friendships—having someone with whom I felt I could be authentic in expressing questions without fearing that this is a situation where I'm dealing with someone who is judging me; someone who has authority over deciding my future and therefore I have to be very careful about what I say; or this is a politically charged situation when a conversation with this individual could possibly have repercussions that would be very, very problematic for me later.

> Friendships have been vital because they have been the place where the heart could be open, where thoughts could flow.

Friendships have been vital because they have been the place where the heart could be open, where thoughts could flow. I could look at myself in ways that perhaps would be less the case in a more formal relationship, either with an authority figure or someone who I was looking to for a formal mentoring relationship.

I will often initiate an outreach of conversation and getting to know one another with a few colleagues who are just coming on board— especially those with whom I feel a strong sense of resonance. To be certain that they are not beginning their time at the school without a colleague they can depend on for conversations, a colleague who can help them understand what's happening in this place, and what the spoken and the unspoken realities are of being a faculty member who is hopefully successfully moving through the process of tenure and relating with colleagues well. This helps them understand institutional expectations, and understand the ways in which an institution can make demands upon you that actually divert you from your sense of vocation. Those realities are part of any institution, including an academic one.

I was eager to be in conversation with Greg just to know him. Over time, what would occur is providing advice about aspects of institutional life. That advice would occur from his asking questions. Sometimes I might initiate a comment or two, but I never really conceived of it as, "I'm mentoring Greg." I understand it as I'm being a friend and a colleague. I have been very honored that Greg would characterize our relationship as my being in a mentoring role for him.

I find myself inspired by Greg's way of exercising his own vocation. I'm energized by it. I think a lot of people characterize mentoring relationships as occurring one-way. It's from the person who's identified as a mentor to the mentee. It's actually a very mutual exchange. There's growth occurring at both ends.

I would even characterize it as spiritual friendship. We're really having

There's a sense in which this is sacred time of being on sacred ground with one another.

exchanges that are more than problem solving, that are more than providing answers to personal questions. There's a sense in which this is sacred time of being on sacred ground with one another. When someone exposes their heart in conversation ... We come out of our time together feeling great anticipation of the next time that we'll be together.

DIVA: Why do you think it's important to mentor rising leaders like Rev. Dr. Greg Ellison?

LUTHER: I think that the interaction with another generation can always be beneficial. It's mind-expanding. It's heart-expanding. If it's with an older generation, you are drawing upon the wisdom of someone who's covered more ground than you have covered. If it's with a younger generation, it's often with someone who has covered different ground, and who is able to give expression to what aligns with the way in which my current generation is seeing things, and what is very different, and how might we begin to translate that difference in ways that enable us to be moving forward together. It's a very informing and energizing experience for me to be relating with those who are younger. It's not just a matter of bringing them along and seeing myself as providing something of the maturation of them. I find myself being matured through these kinds of conversations.

DIVA: When you think about the work that you've done in your life, how does that relate to what Rev. Dr. Ellison's doing, and to how he's helping Rev. Alisha Gordon?

LUTHER: The sort of work that Greg is doing and the sort of work that I've been involved with can be work of intense commitment. While you love intense commitment in terms of the way in which people may give themselves to an organization with time and resources and passion, that can also be the context for increased difficulty or conflict.

To have someone from outside of your context with whom you can be in conversation about what's going on can be extremely helpful. You can talk through matters that feel confidential, that you would dare not try to work through with someone else who's involved in your organization because you would be breaking some levels of confidentiality. Plus you never know how some things you're trying to understand and how you speak to someone might actually be contributing to a problem.

These kinds of relationships can be extremely helpful for an individual to feel that they have a way of attending to the concerns of heart and mind and strategy and personality—without having to risk this exploration in a way that actually damages what they're involved in, rather than in ways that just give them greater insight. Our availability to one another enables us to work through these kinds of matters in ways that contribute to the larger organization in which we're involved.

Hopefully, this becomes a way in which persons can establish mentoring relationships or friendships in a whole range of organizations. One of the things we have taught to pastors who are students in the School of Theology is that you really need to have relationships that enable you to talk about realities within your congregation—and not just with people who are within your congregation. If you try to address all of those issues just with the folks who are in your congregation you can start things that create more turmoil than benefit.

This is true for the kind of work that Greg is doing as he's seeking to effect transformation, both nationally and internationally, with an organization of very committed people.

DIVA: Would you consider Howard Thurman one of your mentors?

LUTHER: Oh, yes. Yes. Howard Thurman has been walking with me for over 40 years now. There are just so many ways in which he continues to be a counsel, to be a companion of the journey. Again, this was not a formal mentoring relationship. My first conversations with Dr. Thurman were through friendship—my feeling this need to just establish a relationship with him, not even with any clear objective as to why this would be important, except that I felt my life would be so enhanced by exploring this urging. Dr. Thurman also then became a subject of scholarship for me. I continue to hear in so many ways the conversations I had with him. He's also been speaking to me through his writings and through his public speaking. That has been very important to me.

DIVA: With regard to the different relationships that you've had with Howard Thurman and with Rev. Dr. Ellison—and with all the students whose lives you've touched—how does this impact the world for the better? How is it changing the world for good?

LUTHER: I really appreciate the opportunities that occur through technology for communicating with one another, and how that even forms some elements of community among people. But I think there's a real danger that we lose the gift and the value of personal presence with one another. There's a power in that that I don't think gets met through the ways in which we might communicate through email or Facebook or other forms of doing this electronically. When I'm with you, when your presence is available to me and my presence is available to you, it's so very different. What we see through expression

> I think there's a real danger that we lose the gift and the value of personal presence with one another.

is essential—be they expressions of excitement or expressions of doubt; they may not even be expressions that you're wanting to communicate, but they shove themselves forth in body language, in tone of voice, especially when it's an unhurried presence that we have with one another.

Just having the luxury and the privilege of unhurried presence with one another enables the gift of relationship to truly flourish. That's something you cherish. This is sacred time, creating sacred place, sacred relationships. I think the value of that is incalculable. It's so easy for it to be lost to us because of the demands upon us. Just about everyone I know feels exhausted by their work demands, by their play demands, by their family demands. You have to be very intentional to carve out unhurried time for relationships, and be very dedicated to it.

> Having the luxury and the privilege of unhurried presence with one another enables the gift of relationship to truly flourish.

I think that's going to be essential for any kind of ongoing change for which we're looking in society. I don't think you get to beloved community just through ideals or just through massive change. I think you get to beloved community through both personal change and interpersonal change, along with these other expressions of community. If we forfeit personal and interpersonal change to giving our energies solely to the institutional, systemic dimensions of change, I think we've missed a crucial step to beloved community.

The second thing would be tenacity. It's easy to get people disturbed and involved to effect change at a rally, or to say, "We're going to really be working to achieve this within three months." But the kind of changes that Greg is about, the kind of changes that I'm working on in my own life, are changes that are not in any way over at the end of a particular deadline. You win some struggles and you lose some struggles. Even the struggles that you win will often be lost later. You get a legislative change that affects thousands and thousands of people, and you celebrate. You have your parties about it. Then in the next legislative session they begin to cut away at the very thing that has been achieved. You have to have a way of both celebrating gains and coming together and being strengthened in losses and being ready to continue to take the next step. Tenacity is vital to any sort of long-term, ongoing change for beloved community.

That, to me, is essential. When I think about the kind of mentoring relationship that is key to transformations that lead to the beloved community, these are relationships for the long term. This is very different from just talking to a consultant or talking to a therapist. My heart is in it not just for the outcome of this particular issue. My heart is in it because of my relationship with you as well as the larger issues that we're addressing together. That's what it means to be a companion for the journey.

> Tenacity is vital to any sort of long-term, ongoing change for beloved community.

If I had to have a term that most characterizes my understanding of mentoring, it would be "being a companion for the journey," for the *whole* journey. For me, change for good is energizing, which is another way of saying it's life-giving.

For the full video, visit fteleaders.org/stories/lead-generational-change-for-good.